Computer Language H

C Language

Friedman Wagner-Dobler

Pitman

Computer Handbooks

The complete list of titles in this series and the Pitman Pocket Guide series appears after the Index at the end of this Handbook. The Publishers would welcome suggestions for further additions and improvements to the series. Please write to Ian Pringle at the address given below.

PITMAN PUBLISHING LIMITED
128 Long Acre, London WC2E 9AN

A Longman Group Company

© Friedman Wagner-Dobler 1985

First edition 1985, reprinted 1986

British Library Cataloguing in Publication Data

Wagner-Dobler, Friedman
  C Language.—(Computer handbooks)
  1. C (Computer program language)
  I. Title   II. Series
  001.64'24   QA76.73.C15

ISBN 0 273 02246 6

Printed in Great Britain at The Bath Press, Avon

Contents

Publisher's Notes

DEC, PDP, VAX, RMS and VMS are trademarks of Digital Equipment Corporation.

UNIX is a trademark of A. T. & T. Bell Laboratories.

CP/M is a registered trademark of Digital Research Inc.

Microsoft and MS are trademarks of Microsoft Corporation.

Lattice is a registered trademark of Lattice, Inc.

C86 and Optimizing=C86 are trademarks of Computer Innovations, Inc.

How to Use this Handbook

This Handbook describes the C language as implemented on a diverse range of processors and operating systems. In addition to the definition of the language by Kernighan and Ritchie,* ten versions of C have been used for reference purposes. They are listed below, together with the abbreviation used for each.

KR — The C language as defined by Brian W. Kernighan and Dennis M. Ritchie (UNIX) — 1978

U7 — UNIX Version 7 C Compiler — 1979

CR — Cromemco C (8-bit Cromix/CDOS) — February 1981

VAX — VAX 11 C Version 1.0 (RMS) — 1982

*Brian W. Kernighan and Dennis M. Ritchie, *The C Programming Language,* Prentice Hall 1978.

CC — Control-C CC-86 (CP/M-86) — December 1982

DR — Digital Research C Version 1.11 (CP/M-86) — October 1983

CI — Computer Innovations Optimizing=C86 2.00 (MS-DOS and CP/M-86) — December 1983

LAT — Lattice/Microsoft C Version 2.03 (MS-DOS 2.0) — 1984

U5 — UNIX System V Release 2.0 C Compiler — April 1984

DES — DeSMET C Language Version 2.3 (MS-DOS and CP/M-86) — June 1984

MC — Microsoft C Version 3 (MS-DOS 2.1) — not released at time of writing

Occasionally, other C compilers have also been taken into account. Throughout the text, we will use the delta symbol Δ to warn you that a particular feature is not portable across the range.

Notation

Syntax rules
C keywords and examples are set thus:

main() {/* sample program */}

Syntactic categories are printed in *italics*. Items appearing on separate lines are mutually exclusive alternatives. An <*optional element*> is indicated by angle brackets. The horizontal ellipsis '...' indicates optional repetition; if preceded by a comma, the repeated elements must be separated by commas.

Details of the format used to describe the C library are given on pp. 52 ff.

The C Language

Elements

Character set
The C character set is implementation dependent, but a subset is portable. The portable subset consists of graphic characters, whitespace and special characters. Any member of the machine's character set can be expressed with an escape sequence: but escape sequences which involve octal or hexadecimal codes are not portable, except for the NUL character '\0'.

Graphic characters
The term 'graphic character' will be used for characters which are legal in identifiers. This applies to:

- the upper-case letters A . . . Z
- the lower-case letters a . . . z
- the decimal digits 0 . . . 9
- the underscore '_'
- in some implementations, the dollar sign '$'   Δ

Upper- and lower-case letters are distinct, except in hexadecimal constants. The decimal digits are always in ascending and contiguous order.

Special characters
The following special characters are used:

,	comma	%	percent sign
.	period	&	ampersand
;	semicolon	^	caret
:	colon	*	asterisk
?	question mark	−	minus sign
'	apostrophe	=	equal sign
"	quotation mark	+	plus sign
!	exclamation mark	< >	angle brackets
|	vertical bar	()	parentheses
/	slash	[]	brackets
\	backslash	{}	braces
~	tilde	#	number sign

Whitespace
Space, horizontal tab, newline, carriage return, and form feed are collectively considered as whitespace. Some implementations consider end-of-file padding or the vertical tab as whitespace. The compiler ignores whitespace unless it is part of a character or string constant; it is prohibited between the characters of identifiers, multi-character operators and keywords. Sometimes, whitespace is necessary to separate tokens. For instance,

a+++b

means **(a++)+(b)** because the parser tries to assemble the longest possible token (i.e. '++').

a+ ++b

uses whitespace to separate the tokens '+' and '++', and is interpreted as **(a)+(++b)**.

4

Escape sequences

String and character constants (pp. 7–8) may contain escape sequences as shown:

\n	newline	\d	characters with
\t	horizontal tab	\dd	octal codes
\b	backspace	\ddd	d, dd, ddd
\r	carriage return	\xh	characters with hexa-
\f	form feed	\xhh	decimal codes h, hh △
\'	apostrophe (character)	\e	ASCII escape △
\"	quotation mark (string)	\v	vertical tab △
\\	backslash		

The backslash character followed by a newline serves as a continuation character in strings and preprocessor directives. For example:

△   **char *string= "is split over \
   two lines";**

Unfortunately, compiler limitations often make this use non-portable.

Keywords

Keywords cannot be used as identifiers. But they can be redefined in the preprocessor; for instance, #**define void int** will redefine all **void** declarations as **int**.

auto	**else**	**int**	**struct**
break	**enum** △	**long**	**switch**
case	**extern**	**register**	**typedef**
char	**float**	**return**	**union**
continue	**for**	**short**	**unsigned**
default	**goto**	**sizeof**	**void** △
do	**if**	**static**	**while**
double			

Various compilers use additional non-standard keywords; these are included in Table 8 on p. 63.

Comments
Comments are delimited by the character pairs **/*** and ***/**. A comment can appear anywhere that whitespace can appear. Comments do not nest, so **/* this /* is a */ bug */** is seen by the compiler as **bug */**. If program sections containing comments are to be edited out, you should use the preprocessor directives #**if** or #**ifdef**. Thus, if KNOCKIT is an undefined symbol, the sequence

#**ifdef KNOCKIT**
dummy() {/* deep freeze code */}
#**endif**

will correctly get rid of the function **dummy.**

Identifiers
Identifiers are user supplied names for variables, functions and labels. An identifier consists of a sequence of graphic characters, but the following restrictions apply:

● the first character cannot be a digit
● the first eight characters only are significant
● leading and trailing underscores may cause conflict with the name of library functions
● globally visible identifiers suffer from linker limitations: case distinction may be lost, underscores may be illegal, and only the first seven characters may be significant

Identifiers which should be avoided are given on p. 62; the visibility of identifiers is discussed on p. 45. Examples of 'safe' identifiers are:

chkcrc	HalfCnt	nophone
another	amber14	incount
NextR1	lumber	knock
PrevEx	oddity9	identID

Constants

Integer constants
Integer constants may be given in hexadecimal, octal or decimal notation. Hexadecimal constants begin with **0x** or **0X**, octal constants with **0**, decimal constants with the digits **1** through **9**. Any integer constant may be preceded by a minus sign, but there is no unary plus sign. Integer constants which exceed the size of an **int** are converted to **long**. An integer constant followed by the letters **l** or **L** is also converted to **long**. No whitespace is allowed.

Character constants
Character constants are single characters enclosed in apostrophes. Multi-character constants are not portable. Escape sequences (p. 5) are legal. Character constants have type **int**.

String constants

A string, in C, is an array of characters terminated by the NUL character. String constants consist of zero or more characters enclosed in quotation marks. Escape sequences (p. 5) are legal. String constants generate a static array of type **char**; the null character is appended after the last character in the string. Thus,

```
char dog1[ ]="wow";
char dog2[ ]= {'w','o','w','\0'};
char dog3[4]= {'w','o','w','\0'};
```

are all equivalent. When used in an expression, a string constant is treated as the address of its first character. Identically written string constants may or may not be allocated distinct storage: some compilers will allocate twelve characters for three 'wow's, others four. Because **auto** arrays cannot be initialized,

```
main() /* WRONG */
{
    char dog4[ ]="wow";
}
```

is not legal. You may declare dog4 as static:

```
static char dog4[ ]="wow";
```

Alternatively, you can use a pointer to a **static** array (although this will require more storage), with

```
char*dog5="wow";.
```

which creates a **static** array of characters and an **auto** pointer to the array, **dog5**.

Floating point constants
The form of floating point constants is:

$$<->\ <integral\ part>\ <.\ fractional\ part>$$
$$<^{E}_{e}<sign>exponent>$$

At least the integral and exponential parts, or the fractional part, must be present. Whitespace is not allowed. Floating point constants have the type **double**. Examples of legal floating constants are:

```
0.7e5
19e-56
19E+56
351.2106
```

Note that '+351.2106' is not a legal floating point constant because there is no unary plus in C.

Variables and declarations

Data types
The data types of the C language and the terminology used to describe them are summarized in Figure 1.

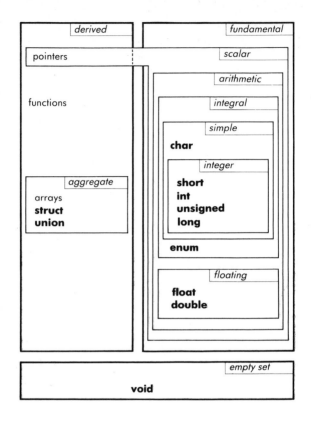

Figure 1 Data types

Arithmetic types

The basic data types of the C language are

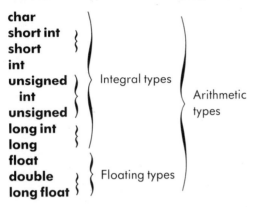

char
short int
short
int
unsigned int
unsigned
long int
long

Integral types

float
double
long float

Floating types

Arithmetic types

Δ Some compilers also allow other short/long/ unsigned compounds (for instance, unsigned char). Most such combinations are not portable; if you have to use them, you should **typedef** them. The size of any of the basic data types, and the storage associated with them, are implementation dependent; see p. 51 for minimum sizes.

Declarations

Declarations specify the storage class, type, name and optional initialization of an object. Table 1 indicates the syntax of a simple declaration.

Table 1 *Simple declarations*

<sc-spec>	<type-spec>	<declarator>	<initializer>;
	char		
	short		
	int		
auto	**long**	id	
static	**unsigned**	*id	
register	**float**	id( )	initializer;
extern	**double**	id[constant_ expr]	
	struct-spec		
	union-spec		
	enum-spec		
	typedef-name		

Pairs of *declarators* and *initializers* may be present in a comma-separated list.

Storage class specifiers
Declarations outside a function imply the default storage **static**. A static variable has storage allocated to it throughout the life of the program, and its value remains the same unless changed by a function: its scope is said to be the program.

The **auto** keyword is redundant in as much as **auto** variables cannot be declared outside a function, and declarations inside the body of a function are assumed to be **auto** anyway. Storage is allocated (on the stack) until the function returns: the scope of an **auto** variable is said to be the function. On some machines, **static** objects are manipulated faster and more efficiently than **auto** objects.

The **register** keyword also creates **auto** objects, but it directs the compiler to store an object in a fast register; it is a hint to the compiler that a variable is used heavily. Current compilers only allow scalar types (but not floating types) to be stored in registers. If no register is available, the keyword will be ignored and the variable is converted to **auto**. You cannot take the address of a **register** variable.

Extern allocates no storage but implies that the declared object is present either later in the source file or in another source file; see p. 45 for a fuller discussion of visibility.

Type specifier
The *type-specifier* indicates the type of the desired object. If the *type-specifier* is omitted, **int** is assumed.

Declarator
An identifier on its own declares that to be the name of the object specified. Thus,

static int x;

declares a static integer named **x**. In addition, asterisks, parentheses and brackets may be used to declare pointers to an object, functions returning an object, and arrays of objects respectively (see pp. 19 ff).

Initializer

There may be a single initializer for each object declared. For instance,

int y=34;

Variable expressions may be used for initialization if the declaration occurs within the body of a function, as in

int z=x+y;

For arrays and structures (unions cannot be initialized), the initializer consists of a brace-enclosed, comma-separated list of initializers for the aggregate's members, written in increasing subscript of member order. This rule may be applied recursively for sub-aggregates. If there are fewer initializers than members, the rest of the aggregate (or sub-aggregate) is padded with zeros. A simple case is

static double x[3] = {1.0, 2.0, 3.0};

The braces may be omitted for sub-aggregates, but note that while

static double y[3][2] = {{1.0}, {1.0}, {1.0}};

initializes **y[0][0]**, **y[1][0]** and **y[2][0]**, the declaration

static double z[3][2] = {1.0, 1.0, 1.0};

initializes **y[0][0]**, **y[0][1]** and **y[1][0]**. Character arrays may be initialized with strings (p. 8).

Use of enumeration, structure and union tags

The syntax for specifying enumerations, structures and unions is identical. That is, there are two forms which may be used. First, the compound type may be completely declared *in situ*, with or without a tag. Thus, in Table 1

enum <*tag*> {*whatever*} is an *enum-spec*
struct <*tag*> {*whatever*} is a *struct-spec*
union <*tag*> {*whatever*} is a *union-spec*

If the *tag* is given, then it may subsequently be used to replace the complete definition, thus

enum *tag* becomes an *enum-spec*
struct *tag* becomes a *struct-spec*
union *tag* becomes a *union-spec*

Enumerations

Δ Enumerations are not legal in many compilers. They define a set of values and should be seen as a type distinct from the integral types, although an enumeration variable has most of the properties of an **int**. The syntax of an *enumeration-specifier* is:

enum <*tag*> <{*enum-list*}>

with *enum-list* taking the form

identifier <= *constant-expression*> ,...

Each *identifier* names a value of the enumeration set.
The first value is assumed to be 0; each subsequent
value is assumed to be the previous value plus one.
These assignments are overridden if a *constant-
expression* is present. Thus,

enum {red, green, blue} x = red;

allocates storage for an enumerated variable **x**
which can have the values red, green or blue (0, 1 or
2), and

enum {red=−1, green, blue} y = red;

creates a similar variable which takes the values −1,
0 and 1. It is possible for an enumeration set to
contain duplicate constant values, but it may not
contain duplicate identifiers. The scope of
enumeration identifiers is the same as and conflicts
with ordinary variable names. Thus,

int green;

would conflict with the examples above in the same
scope. Only the assignment operator =, and the
logical operators == and **!**= are legal for
enumeration variables.

Structures
A structure is a sequence of variable values which
can have different types. The syntax of a *structure-
specification* is

struct<*tag*> <{*member-declaration-list*}>

where the *member-declaration-list* is a list of one or more variables or bitfield declarations. Structures with storage class **auto** cannot be initialized. Δ In some implementations, structures may be assigned, and can be passed to or returned from functions.

Structure members — variables
Structure members may be variables of any type, but a structure cannot contain an instance of itself. Thus, if **bug** is the tag of a structure,

struct bug {int x; struct bug y;}

is a bug. But you can use pointers to the same structure:

struct nobug {int x; struct nobug *y;}

Structure members are referred to by means of the period, as in

nobug.x

which refers to member **x** of the structure (in this case, an **int**). If **ps** is a pointer to **nobug**, then

(*ps).x

refers to the same object. The parentheses are necessary because the period operator ('member') has higher precedence than the unary asterisk ('pointer to') operator. A more convenient and completely equivalent alternative is to write

ps−>x

where the token −> is formed by a combination of minus sign and right-angle bracket.

Structure members — bitfields

To be portable, bitfield declarations should have the form

unsigned <*identifier*> **:** *field-width***;**

where *field-width* is a positive constant expression no larger than the number of bits in an **unsigned int**. Bitfields are not stored across **int** boundaries; pointers to, arrays of, and functions returning bitfields are illegal. Bitfields are useful to conserve storage. For instance,

struct {**int red; int blue; int green; int bright;**}

requires four **ints** in storage, while

struct {**unsigned red:1, blue:1, green:1, bright:1;**}

requires only one **int**. Bitfields are referred to like structure members and they cannot be initialized.

Unions

Union declarations define a variable which contains exactly one variable of a set of different variables. Union declarations have the same form as structure declarations, but they begin with the **union** keyword; bitfields are not allowed in unions. For instance,

union struct {**int i; float f;** } **both;**

declares a union which stores either an **int** or a **float**. It is up to you to keep track of what is currently stored in a union; thus,

```
int x;
. . .
both.f=12.34;
x=both.i;
```

will assign an undefined value to x. Unions cannot be
initialized, even if they have storage class **static**.

Pointers
An asterisk which prefixes an identifier in a
declaration declares an object of type 'pointer to'.
Thus,

char c;

declares an object of type **char** while

char ∗c;

declares an object of type 'pointer to an object of
type **char**'.
  Pointers may point to any variable, but not to
bitfields or **register** variables. A subset of
arithmetic operations may be performed on pointers.
Integers may be added to or subtracted from
pointers (incrementation and decrementation are
special cases); the meaning of the expression

```
char ∗p;
p=p+1;
```

is 'point to the next object of type char' and, for the resulting pointer to be meaningful and portable, it must be guaranteed that the next object in storage is also a **char**. This is only the case when a pointer points to an array. A pointer may be assigned to another pointer, or to an **int** providing it is large enough (**long** always is, a plain **int** may not be). Pointers may be compared for equality to other pointers, or to NULL; it is guaranteed that the NULL pointer does not point to any valid object. Pointers to elements of the same array may be subtracted.

Type punning is always machine dependent. It is not necessarily true that a pointer to an object of one type has the same size as a pointer to an object of another type. NULL pointers which are passed to a function should be coerced to the correct type. Thus,

execl ("myprog", "-bug",NULL)

will fail on some systems because it passes the integer NULL to **execl**; what is required is an explicit cast, as in

execl ("myprog", "-bug", (char*)0)

This is preferable to declaring a null pointer (e.g. NULLPTR) because (for instance) a pointer to a function may have a size which is different from the size of a pointer to **char**.

Arrays
An identifier postfixed by brackets and a constant expression declares an object of type 'array of . . .'. Thus

char x[100];

declares an array of 100 **char**s. Arrays which have storage class **auto** cannot be initialized. As a special case of the recursive creation of new data types,

char x[25][80];

creates an array of dimensions 25 by 80. Arrays are stored row wise, that is

char x[0][0. . . 79]
char x[1][0. . . 79]

are guaranteed to be contiguous.

Function declarations
An identifier postfixed by empty parentheses declares an object of type 'function returning . . .'. Thus,

float x();

declares a function **x** which returns an object of type **float**. Δ Functions may be declared with type **void**, which means that the function does not return a value and that it is erroneous to use a return value. Functions may return arithmetic types, enumerations, pointers, and in some later implementations Δ structures. They can only have the storage classes **extern** or **static**. If the compiler encounters a previously undefined identifier followed by a left parenthesis, it will contextually declare it to be a function returning **int**: hence, forward references to such functions are allowed. Forward references to functions which do not return an **int** must be declared explicitly.

It is not possible to write a portable function with a variable number of arguments. The order of evaluation of the arguments to a function is undefined, that is

func(x,y) int x,y; {. . .}
int a=1;
func (++a,++a)

is not reliable and might result in x being 2 and y being 3, or vice versa. Function arguments are always coerced into one of the types **int**, **long**, **double**, *pointer to* or Δ structure before the call. It does not matter, therefore, whether you call a function with a **float** or a **double**, or (subject to possible sign extension) a **char** or an **int**.

Δ The ANSI Standards Committee (X3J11) for C has defined the ability to do type checking on function arguments (currently only implemented in MC). This means that the compiler can issue warnings when the arguments of a function should be different from the actual parameters, and can detect mismatches in the number of actual parameters and formal parameters; the compiler can also coerce actual parameters when a type mismatch occurs.

The syntax defined for type checking is as for types. For example:

Δ **int check(int,double);**

declares that **check** takes two parameters and that they are of type **int** and **double** respectively. The special case of a function without parameters is declared as

△ **int noparf (void);**

which is different from

int nocheck ();

which is the old syntax and disables any checking the compiler might otherwise do. Functions which take a variable number of arguments can be declared as

△ **int vararg (char *,);**

In the example given, **vararg** has one parameter of type pointer to **char**, and any number of unknown (and unchecked) type arguments (the library function **printf** might be declared in this way).

Complex declarations
In general, all the declarations listed above may be applied recursively. The following is an easy manual method to generate complex declarations.

(1) Write down the declaration in English, using the expressions 'pointer to . . .', 'function returning . . .', and 'array of . . .' only (e.g. 'function returning pointer to an array of pointers to structures').

(2) Write down the type at the left, the name in the middle, and the semicolon at the right, e.g.

   struct sample   x   ;

(3) Working your way from the right hand of the sentence, replace the term in the middle

   with *(term) for 'pointer to'
   with (term) () for 'function returning'
   with (term) **[]** for 'array of'

In our example (a function returning pointer to an array of pointers to structures), this gives:

struct sample	*(**x**)	;
struct sample	(*(**x**))[ ]	;
struct sample	*((*(**x**))[ ])	;
struct sample	(*((*(**x**))[ ]))()	;

A similar method may be used to reduce complex declarations:

(1) Bear in mind that the primary operators **[ ]** and **( )** have higher precedence than the unary *, and group left to right (i.e. remove the rightmost **[ ]** or **( )** first if there is a combination of these operators). The unary * groups right to left; parentheses may change the order of binding.

(2) Write down

'function returning' instead of **( )**
'array of' instead of **[ ]**
'pointer to' instead of *

and drop the corresponding element from the declaration.

(3) Repeat step 2 until only the identifier is left, and you have the identifier's description.

Table 2 lists the most common complex declarations up to five levels of nesting. It can be used simply by substitution; taking the first entry as an example,

struct test *x[ ];

declares x to be an array of pointer to a structure tagged **test**.

Table 2   *Complex declarations*

Second degree

*x[]	array of pointers to
*x()	function returning pointer to
(*x)[]	pointer to array of
(*x)()	pointer to function returning

Third degree

(*x[])[]	array of pointers to arrays of
(*x[])()	array of pointers to functions returning
(*x())[]	function returning pointer to array of
(*x())()	function returning pointer to function returning
*(*x)[ ]	pointer to array of pointers to
*(*x)()	pointer to function returning pointer to

Fourth degree

*(*x[])[]	array of pointers to arrays of pointers to
*(*x[])()	array of pointers to functions returning pointers to
*(*x())[]	function returning pointer to array of pointers to
*(*x())()	function returning pointer to function returning pointer to
(*(*x)[])[]	pointer to array of pointers to arrays of
(*(*x)[])()	pointer to array of pointers to functions returning
(*(*x)())[]	pointer to function returning pointer to array of
(*(*x)())()	pointer to function returning pointer to function returning

Table 2   *Complex declarations (continued)*

Fifth degree

(*(*x[])[])[]	array of pointers to arrays of pointers to arrays of
(*(*x[])[])()	array of pointers to arrays of pointers to function returning
(*(*x[])())[]	array of pointers to function returning pointers to arrays of
(*(*x[])())()	array of pointers to function returning pointers to function returning
(*(*x())[])[]	function returning pointer to array of pointers to arrays of
(*(*x())[])()	function returning pointer to array of pointers to functions returning
(*(*x())())[]	function returning pointer to function returning pointer to array of
(*(*x())())()	function returning pointer to function returning pointer to function returning
((*x)[])[]	pointer to array of pointers to arrays of pointers to
((*x)[])()	pointer to array of pointers to function returning pointers to
((*x)())[]	pointer to function returning pointer to array of pointers to
((*x)())()	pointer to function returning pointer to function returning pointer to

Typedefs

Typedefs may be used to create new data type names. This is useful to parameterize programs against portability problems and to simplify non-intuitive declarations like

float *(*x())();

Syntactically, **typedef** appears in place of the storage class and the name of the new data type in place of the declared object. Hence,

typedef float *(*MYTYPE())();

allows you to use **MYTYPE** to declare functions returning pointers to functions returning pointers to **floats**, and

extern MYTYPE a,b,c;

becomes

extern float *(*a ())(), *(*b())(), *(*c())();

A number of **typedef**s may be combined, as in

typedef char *STRING, *SFUNC(),
*(*SFARR[])();

which defines three new types, strings (pointers to **char**), functions returning strings, and arrays of pointers to functions returning strings.

Expressions and operators

Figure 2 lists the operators of the C language and their precedence. No whitespace is allowed between characters of multi-character operators.

Category	Operator	Associativity
primary	( ) [ ] . ->	left to right
unary	* & ++ -- ~ - **sizeof** *(type-name)* !	right to left
binary	* / %	left to right
	+ -	
	<< >>	
	< > <= >=	
	== !=	
	&	
	^	
	¦	
	&&	
	¦¦	
conditional	?:	right to left
assignment	= += -= *= /= %= >>= <<= &= ^= ¦=	
comma	,	left to right

Logical operators are shaded.

Figure 2 Operator classes and precedence

Primary operators

The primary operators have already been dealt with on pp. 21 (functions), 20 (arrays) and 17 (structure and union members).

Logical operators

C deems the numeric value 0 to be false, any other numeric value to be true. Logical operators always produce a value of type **int**: 1 for true and 0 for false. Their meaning is given in Table 3; braces indicate an equal level of precedence. (Note that the term 'logical operators' is often used in a more restrictive sense to refer to the operators **&&** and **||** only.)

Table 3   *Logical operators*

Operator	Example	Result
!	**!a**	1 if a is 0, otherwise 0
<	**a<b**	1 if a<b, otherwise 0
<=	**a<=b**	1 if a<=b, otherwise 0
>	**a>b**	1 if a>b, otherwise 0
>=	**a>=b**	1 if a>=b, otherwise 0
==	**a==b**	1 if a equal b, otherwise 0
!=	**a!=b**	1 if a not equal to b, otherwise 0
&&	**a&&b**	1 if a and b are true, otherwise 0
||	**a||b**	1 if a is true (b is not evaluated), otherwise 1 if b is true, otherwise 0

Other operators
Table 4 gives details of operators other than primary and logical operators; braces indicate equal levels of precedence. *lv* in the *Example* column indicates that the expression must be an lvalue. The letter i in the penultimate column indicates that the operator expects integral values as operand(s).

Casts
The cast operator (*type*) forces the conversion of its operand to a specified data type. In simple cases, the *type* is just the keyword for a data type, as in

(long) 5

which is the same as

5l or **5L**

In more complex cases, the *type* is the declaration of that type with the identifier omitted (i.e. an *abstract-declarator*). Thus, if

int (∗pai) [ ] ;

declares **pai** to be a pointer to an array of **int**, then

(int (∗)[ ]) 0

is a *NULL* pointer to an array of **int**.

The sizeof operator
The expression **sizeof** (*type*) results in an unsigned integer constant representing the size in bytes of an object of the named *type*. The syntax of *type* is that given for casts. When applied to an array, the **sizeof** operator yields size (in bytes) of the array.

Table 4   *Other operators*

Operator	Example	Result	See p.
~	~a	one's complement of a	i
++	++lv	lv after increment	
	lv++	lv before increment	
--	--lv	lv after decrement	
	lv--	lv before increment	
-	-a	negative of a (two's complement)	
()	(*type*)a	a converted to *type*	30
*	*p	object pointed to by p	
&	&lv	address of object lv	
sizeof	**sizeof** e	size (in bytes) of e	
	sizeof (t)	size (in bytes) of t	
*	a*b	a multiplied by b	
/	a/b	a divided by b	
%	a%b	a modulo b	i
+	a+b	a plus b	
-	a-b	a minus b	
<<	a<<b	a left shifted b bits	i
>>	a>>b	a right shifted b bits	i
&	a&b	bitwise AND of a and b	i
^	a ^ b	bitwise XOR of a and b	i
|	a|b	bitwise OR of a and b	i
?:	a?e1:e2	e1 if a is true, else e2	32
=	lv=b	lv, with b assigned to lv	
+=	lv+=b	lv, lv=lv+b	
-=	lv-=b	lv, lv=lv-b	
*=	lv*=b	lv, lv=1v*b	
/=	lv/=b	lv, lv=1v/b	
%=	lv%=b	lv, lv=1v%b	i
>>=	lv>>=b	lv, lv=lv>>b	i
<<=	lv<<=b	lv, lv=lv<<b	i

31

Table 4 *Other operators (continued)*

Operator	Example	Result	l See p.
&=	lv&=b	lv, lv=lv&b	i
^=	lv ^ =b	lv, lv=lv ^ b	i
|=	lv|=b	lv, lv=lv|b	i
,	e1,e2	e2 (e1 evaluated first)	33

The conditional operator

The ternary conditional operator **?:** tests its first operand. If the first operand is true (not 0), the second operand is evaluated, otherwise the third operand is evaluated. Thus, the expression

e1 **?** *e2* **:** *e3*

becomes

e2

if *e1* is true, otherwise

e3

The usual arithmetic conversions are performed on *e2* and *e3*.

The comma operator

The binary comma operator evaluates the first operand and discards the result. The second operand is then evaluated, and that is the result. Thus,

b++,c

increments **b** and has the value **c**. The type of the result is that of the second operand. If the comma operator appears in a comma-separated list, it must be parenthesized, so

func((b++,c));

is a call to **func** with the single argument **c**.

The usual arithmetic conversions

The usual arithmetic conversions can be expressed in pidgin C as follows:

Convert any **float** operand to **double**;
IF (one operand has type **double**)
    convert the other operand to **double**;
ELSE
    convert any **char** to **int**;
    convert any **short** to **int**;
    IF (one operand is a **long**)
        convert the other operand to **long**;
    ELSE
        IF (one operand is **unsigned**)
            convert the other operand to
            unsigned;
        ELSE
            both operands are **int**;

The rule is more complicated for compilers which allow other **unsigned** quantities. Furthermore, since a pointer could be equivalent to an **int** or a **long**, code which uses knowledge of the size of a pointer may fail on one machine but not another.

Conversions and sign extension
A shorter quantity of type **int** is converted to a longer integral quantity by sign-extension, but if its type is **unsigned**, zero-padding is used. Δ Unexpected results may occur if **long** and **unsigned int** have the same size.

Δ Characters may be used wherever an **int** is used, and may or may not suffer sign extension. This is a major nuisance which needs to be watched carefully.

Longer integral quantities are converted to shorter integral quantities by truncation on the left.

All floating arithmetic is carried out in double-precision. Rounding takes place when a **double** is converted to **float**; no precision is lost when converting **float** to **double**. Conversion of integral values to floating values is well behaved, but loss of precision may occur. No sensible treatment of fractions should be assumed in conversions of floating values to integral values; the result is undefined if the destination lacks sufficient bits.

The library functions **ceil**, **floor**, **frexp**, **ldexp** and **modf** alleviate some of these conversion problems.

Order of evaluation

The precedence and associativity of operators is given in Fig. 2 on p. 28. Otherwise the order of evaluation is undefined. The compiler is free to compute subexpressions in any order without regard to side effects. Thus,

a[i++]=b[i++];

may or may not have the desired effect. Expressions involving the commutative and associative operators *, +, | and ^ may be rearranged, so in the expression

fa(x)+fb(x)

the compiler is free to evaluate **fb** first and then **fa**, even if side-effects are involved. More generally, the result of any expression which re-uses a variable changed by a side-effect should be considered undefined.

Function arguments

Function arguments of type **float** are converted to **double** before the call. Arguments of type **char** or **short** are converted to **int**. Array names (including quoted strings) are converted to pointers to the first element of the array.

△ Some compilers apply the same rule to structure names. Assume there is a structure declared as

struct mixup {int a; int b;};

then

fcall (&mixup)

safely calls **fcall** with a pointer to the structure, but some compilers (of those which do not recognize structures as function arguments) will silently convert

fcall (mixup) Δ

to the first form, although what is probably intended is that **fcall** should be called with a copy of **mixup**.

Statements

Statements and expressions
You can use any expression as a statement by terminating it with a semicolon. For instance,

a=3

is an expression and

a=3;

is a statement. This has the undesirable effect that obviously nonsensical statements are legal:

a+3;

is valid but all it does is to add **a** to **3** and then throw away the result. Some compilers, and the UNIX *lint* utility, will complain, others will not. Equally problematic is

*p++;

which increments the pointer **p** (because + + has higher precedence than *), produces the value pointed to by **p** and blissfully throws it away. Be careful.

Blocks

A block allows more than one statement to appear where a single statement is required. A block statement has the form

{<*declaration-list*> <*statement-list*>}

Declaration-list is a list of declarations local to the block. Previous declarations of variables with the same name are suspended in the inner block, so

```
int d=9;
main ()
{
    int d=12;
    {
            int d=15;
            /* d is 15 */
    }
    /* d is 12 */
}
/* d is 9 */
```

is legal. No declarations are allowed after the first statement.

If and else

A conditional statement has the form

if (*expression*) *statement* < **else** statement>

If *expression* is non-zero, the first *statement* is executed, otherwise (if the **else** clause is present) the second *statement* is executed. For instance,

```
if (a==3)
    printf("Variable a is three\n");
else
    printf("A is not three\n");
```

In a series of **if-else** clauses, **else** matches the most recent **if**.

While
The **while** statement has the form:

while (*expression*) *statement*

The *expression* is evaluated before each execution, and the *statement* is executed zero or more times as long as *expression* is non-zero. Thus,

```
int c=10;
while (c>=0)
{
        printf("%d\n",c);
        c--;
}
```

counts down from 10 to 0. A **break** in the *statement* will pass control to the following statement. A **continue** will pass control to the next *expression* evaluation.

Do . . . while
The **do** statement has the form

do *statement* **while** (*expression*);

The *expression* is evaluated after each execution, and *statement* is executed one or more times until *expression* is zero. For instance, to count spaces from the standard input you could write

```
int c, nsp;
do
{
   c=getchar();
   if (c=='') nsp++;
} while (c!=EOF);
printf ("%d spaces\n");
```

A **break** in the statement will pass control to the following statement. A **continue** will pass control to the next *expression* evaluation.

For

The **for** statement has the form

for (*<e1>* ; *<e2>* ; *<e3>*) *statement*

where *e1*, *e2* and *e3* are *expressions*. The **for** statement is equivalent to

```
e1 ;
while (e2)
{
        statement
CONT:   e3 ;
}
```

with the proviso that a **continue** in the *statement* transfers control to the label CONT. Any of the expressions may be omitted. If *e2* is omitted, the test is always true, hence

for (*e1* **;;** *e3*) *statement*

is an infinite loop which can only be terminated by **break**, **return** or **goto**. A **break** will pass control to the following statement. A **continue** will pass control to the next execution of *e3*.

A typical use of **for** is

```
#define NEL 100
float x[NEL];
int i;
for (i=0;i<NEL;i++)
    x[i]=99.0;
```

which initializes the entire array **x** with the floating point value 99.0.

Switch

The **switch** statement has the form

switch (*expression*) *switch-block*

where *switch-block* is a *block* in which the *declaration-list* does not contain **auto** or **register** variables. Within a *switch-block*, there may be *case-labels*, whose syntax is

case *constant-expression* **:**

The **switch** integer *expression* is evaluated and if it matches any of the *constant-expressions* in a *case-label*, the statement following the label is executed. If there is no matching *constant-expression*, control passes to the statement following the *switch-block*, unless the block contains the

default :

label. In this case, control passes to the statement following the **default :**. No two *case-labels* in the same block may have *constant-expressions* with the same value.

If control reaches any statement in the *switch-loop*, it proceeds sequentially from there on. The **break** statement may be used to pass control to the statement following the *switch-block*. The **continue** statement never refers to a **switch** but may be used to control execution of enclosing **do**, **while** or **for** loops. The following example illustrates a typical use of **switch** (without any attempt to process errors returned by **gets**):

```
char answer [100];
char *gets();
printf("Please answer Yes or No");
gets(answer);
switch (answer[0])
{
   case 'Y':
   case 'y': printf("\nYou answered YES\
             n");
             break;
   case 'N':
   case 'n': printf("\nYou answered No\n");
             break;
   default : printf("\nPlease try again\n");
             break;
```

Break and continue — summary
You can use the **break** statement for **switch**
statements and **do**, **while** and **for** loops. You can
use the **continue** statement only to terminate **do**,
while and **for** loops. The flow of control is shown in
Figure 3; the solid circle indicates the destination of
a **break**.

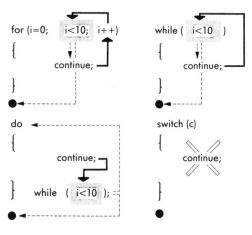

Figure 3

Return
The **return** statement has the form:

return <*expression*> ;

It causes immediate return from a function; if *expression* is present, then it is converted to the type with which the function was declared and returned to the calling function. If no *expression* is given, the return value is undefined; the same applies if a function terminates without a **return**. For instance,

```
cvt(d)
int d;
{
        if ((d>='0') && (d<='9'))
                return (d-'0');
}
```

returns garbage unless **d** is a digit.

Goto
The **goto** statement has the form:

goto *identifier* ;

where *identifier* refers to a label. A label has the form

identifier **:**

and can precede any statement. Its scope is the current function; you cannot jump from one function to another (but see **setjmp** and **longjmp** in the Library section). It is allowed to jump into an inner block in the same function, but if the label does not precede the *declaration-list* of that block, any initializations of **auto** or **register** variables will not have been performed. Thus the following code is suspect:

```
func()
{
    goto noval;
    {
        int x=12;
    noval:; /* x is undefined */
    }
}
```

Null statement
The null statement

```
;
```

is allowed and is often used after a **for** loop when all the work has already been done in the loop itself.

Identifiers revisited

Visibility

It is important to understand the difference between the scope of a variable and the visibility, or 'lexical scope', of identifiers. The scope of a variable is **static** or **local** and indicates its lifespan (see p. 12). An identifier is said to be visible if its type and name are known at a particular point in a source file.

Labels are visible in the entire function in which they are declared, even if they occur in an inner block. Forward references to labels are allowed.

The rules for variables, functions, **enum** constants and **typedef** names are:

● The visibility of an identifier defined outside any function, and the visibility of functions itself, is the rest of the source file. For the purposes of visibility, #**include** files are part of the source file.
● The visibility of an identifier defined in a block is the rest of that block, including nested blocks.
● The visibility of a formal parameter to a function is the entire body of the function.
● Forward references are not allowed. In practice, there is an exception in that forward references to a function returning **int** are allowed: when the compiler encounters an unknown identifier followed by a left parenthesis, the identifier is contextually declared as **extern int id();**

● Variables and functions of scope **static** are
visible to other source files in the same program if
they are declared as **extern** in those source files
(note, again, the exception relating to function
declarations). External variables and functions
which are explicitly declared as **static** are not
visible outside their source file. The apparent
ambiguity of the **static** keyword is resolved if you
consider that it does not make sense to have an
auto variable visible outside a function, because
it does not exist there.

Conflict of variable names
There are four classes of identifiers which do not
conflict with each other, summarized in Figure 4.

structure tags,	ordinary	structure	labels
enum tags,	identifiers,	member	
union tags	function names,	names,	
	enum constants,	union member	
	typedef names	names	

Figure 4   Classes of identifiers

The preprocessor

Conceptually, the C preprocessor is a filter which is
executed before the compiler. It performs textual
substitution, inclusion of files, and is capable of
conditional processing. All preprocessor directives
begin with the number sign # which should occur at
the beginning of a line.

#define

There are two forms of the #**define** directive. The first is

#**define** *identifier* < *token-string*>

and causes *identifier* to be replaced by the *token-string* wherever it occurs in the source file. If no *token-string* is given, the *identifier* is effectively omitted from the source file. The second form of the #**define** directive is

#**define** *identifier* (*identifier ,. . .*) < *token-string*>

No whitespace is allowed between the first identifier and the left parenthesis. This form is capable of more complex substitutions; thus

#**define min(A,B) A**<**B? A:B**

defines an in-line substitution for the expression **min(a,b)** which results in the smaller of the two arguments. Because you are dealing with textual substitution, the arguments of the macro can be any type for which the operations are legal. There are, however, two problems. First, a macro may have side-effects; thus, **min(++a,b)** expands to

++a<**b ? ++a : b**

which does more than it is supposed to do. Second, because an identifier may be replaced by an expression containing operators, it is wise to parenthesize each identifier. Thus

#**define min(A,B) ((A)**<**(B)?(A):(B))**

is much safer and will correctly deal with, for instance,

x +min(a+b,c+d)

#**defines** may be nested.

#undef
The #**undef** directive undefines (makes the preprocessor forget) a previously defined identifier. It is generally agreed that the preprocessor remembers and forgets things in a stacked fashion, so after

#**define SIZE 100**
#**define SIZE 200**
#**undef SIZE**

SIZE is defined as 100. The #**undef** directive undefines previously declared identifiers, whether the first or second form of #**define** was used.

#include
The **include** directive has the form

#**include** "*filename*" or
#**include** < *filename*>

The line is replaced with the entire contents of *filename*. The two different forms may or may not be treated identically. In either case, the files referenced to are obtained from some predetermined place in the file system; the first form probably searches your own directory first. Local conventions apply. As a general rule, use the angle brackets to include system-wide files such as

#**include** <**stdio.h**>

but use the quotation marks to include files which are project specific, as in

#**include "dogfood.h"**

#**include** files can be nested.

#if, #else, #endif
The conditional #**if** directive has the form

*#**if** restricted-constant-expression*
code1
<#**else**
code2 >
#**endif**

If the constant expression evaluates as true, the section *code1* is effective, otherwise section *code2* is effective. #**if**s can be nested. The *restricted-constant-expression* is a *constant-expression* which may not contain **sizeof**.

#ifdef, #ifndef
#**ifdef** and #**ifndef** may appear in place of the #**if** directive; their syntax is

#**ifdef** *identifier*

If the *identifier* is (not) defined, the directive is equivalent to #**if 1**. Some compilers allow the equivalent forms

Δ #**if defined** *identifier* and
Δ #**if !defined** *identifier*

#line
The form of the #**line** directive is

#**line** *constant* " *filename*"

It directs the compiler to issue its error messages referencing the indicated line number and filename. It is typically used only by translators and other preprocessors.

Limitations

Table 5 lists the minimum variable sizes encountered as well as practical compiler limitations.

Table 5 *Limitations*

Type	Size	Range
char	8 bits	0 . . . 255 or −128 . . . 127
int	16 bits	−32768 . . . 32767
short	16 bits	−32768 . . . 32767
unsigned	16 bits	0 . . . 65535
long	32 bits	−2147483648 . . . 2147483647

Type	Precision	Range
float	6 digits	±1.0E±36
double	13 digits	±1.0E±36

Compiler limitations

Maximum source code line length:	128 characters
Maximum **union** size:	76 members
#**include** nesting:	3 levels
printf buffer length:	128 characters
Number of function parameters:	32 parameters
Length of " . . ." strings:	79 characters
Maximum linkable program:	300 externals
switch statement:	32 cases
while/do/for nesting:	10 levels

The Library

Language and library
The C language itself does not define Input or
Output. These facilities are contained in the library,
which is a collection of #**include** library files and
object library functions. There is a reasonable
degree of standardization. The main troublespots on
non-UNIX systems are opening files, the end-of-file,
and processing non-text files.

The function 'main'
A certain amount of system-dependent (but
transparent) processing is performed before a C
program is executed. By convention, the start-up
routine then executes a function called **main**, which
might look like this:

```
main(argc,argv,envp)
int argc;
char *argv[ ];
char *envp[ ];
{
    while(--argc>0)
            procarg(*++argv);
}
```

The first argument is the count of parameters passed to the program by the calling process (typically the shell). The second argument is an array of pointers to strings which represent the arguments passed. Under UNIX (but typically not on other systems), the first of these strings is the name of the called program; the other strings are the program arguments. For instance, if the user types **cat one two**, then

```
argc        is 3
argv[0]     points to the string 'cat'        Δ
argv[1]     points to the string 'one'
argv[2]     points to the string 'two'
```

The third argument of the main function, **envp**, is typically only available under UNIX and is an array of pointers to environment strings such as **PATH=:/bin:/usr/bin**. Note that **main()**, **main(argc)**, and **main(argc,argv)** are also allowed.

Conventions
The header for each library function or macro is given thus:

①	②	③	④	⑤	⑥
double	**fabs**(x)		math	function	math.h
double x; ⑦				⑧ Δ KR CR LAT	

① indicates the type of the return value (**double**). A return value of **void** means that the function does not return a value.
② gives the name of the function (fabs).

③ gives sample arguments for the function. Some common arguments have been given special names, so that they need not be explained for each function. These are shown on page 55.

④ indicates the library type of the function (math.h). This is of relatively little interest outside UNIX. Possible entries are *system* (for UNIX system calls), *math* (for the maths library), *library* for general-purpose library functions and *standard* for general-purpose functions which are listed as part of the Standard I/O library in *UNIX programming* by Kernighan and Ritchie (UNIX programmer's manual, vol. 2, pp. 301–22).

⑤ indicates whether the item in question is a macro or a function. Items declared as macros may in fact be implemented as functions: but it is wiser to assume that you are dealing with a macro. Macros may have side-effects and you cannot take their address.

⑥ indicates the header file which should be #**included**. This is mandatory except for the files *math.h* and *string.h* which merely declare the appropriate functions as **extern**s with the appropriate return value to save you work.

⑦ gives the types of the arguments. Because of the conversion rules for functions, arguments of types **float** and **double** are interchangeable.

⑧ lists the compilers for which this function is not implemented, so you can judge for yourself how risky it is to use the function.

All functions which were common to at least six out of the eleven compilers (counting the Kernighan and Ritchie book and paper as one) have been included, though some minor exceptions were made. We have tried to describe the consensus of compilers: but occasionally one which was obviously delinquent was ignored.

Common arguments
Some arguments are common to a number of functions, and they will not be explained for each. They have been given names which are specific to this handbook and are:

Fpath   A string designating a filename or file path, e.g.

char *Fpath = "Myfile";

Dpath   A string designating a directory path, e.g.

char *Dpath = "usr/bin";

StreamP   A pointer to an object of type FILE (which is declared in stdio.h). File pointers are used to refer to buffered streams. Note that the predefined names **stdin**, **stdout** and **stderr** are constant file pointers. File pointers may be declared as

FILE * filp;

| Handle | File pointers refer to streams; a handle, or file descriptor, is a small positive integer which refers to an unbuffered file opened with one of the system calls, e.g. |

int handle;
handle=open("Myfile",mode);

It is a ghastly error to use a StreamP in place of a Handle, or vice versa.

Pfmt	**printf** format string
Plst	**printf** argument list
Sfmt	**scanf** format string
Slst	**scanf** argument list

see page 57

Error returns
Most functions have some sort of error return, which is usually −1. In many cases, the external **int** variable

errno

is set to an error number indicating the precise nature of the error; the possible error numbers are defined in file *errno.h.* Only two specific errors occur in the alphabetic library listing:

| EDOM | the argument passed was out of the domain of a maths function |
| ERANGE | the result of a calculation was too large |

Use of the library function **perror** or some such stratagem is recommended for unexpected errors.

Formatted output (printf)
The **printf** family of calls is listed as

printf(Pfmt,Plst)

where Pfmt is the format control string and Plst a comma-separated list of arguments.

Pfmt may contain characters which are written literally to the output specified. Thus,

printf("Hello, world\n");

prints the string to **stdout**. Pfmt may also contain format specifications, which begin with the percent sign %; see Table 6 on p. 58 for a complete list. An example is

char *s="hello";
printf("Hello, %s\n",s);

For each format specification (Δ or asterisk in one) in Pfmt, there must be exactly one argument of the proper type in Plst, otherwise havoc may ensue.

Formatted input (scanf)
The **scanf** family of calls is listed as

scanf(Sfmt,Slst)

where Sfmt is the scan control string and Slst a comma-separated list of arguments which **must all be pointers**.

Table 6 *Format specifications*

A print format specification has the form:

% <*flags*> <<0> <*width*>> <.> <*precision*> <l> *conv-char*

flags	'−' left-justifies the converted output in its field.
	'+' Δ forces a sign ('+' or '−') for signed conversions
	' ' Δ forces a sign (' ' or '−') for signed conversions
	'#' Δ forces a leading 0, 0x, or 0. where appropriate
0	specifies that padding should take place with zeros instead of spaces
width	is an integer constant which specifies the minimum field width. Output is right justified unless over-ridden. A converted value exceeding *width* is written out anyway
	separates *width* and *precision*
precision	is an integer constant which specifies the maximum number of string characters to print (format s), or the number of fractional digits (formats e and f)
l or L	specify that the corresponding variable is **long**

Δ Some libraries allow an asterisk to replace *width* or *precision*; in this case, a corresponding **int** must be in the output list. The *conversion-characters* are:

Char	Argument	Action
d	int	convert to decimal format
o	int	convert to octal format, without a leading 0

Table 6 *Format specifications (continued)*

Char Argument Action

x	int	convert to unsigned hexadecimal format, without a leading 0x. Hexadecimal digits may be upper or lower case
u	int	convert to unsigned decimal format
c	char/int	output as a single character (NUL characters may be ignored)
s	*char	output as character string. If *precision* is omitted or 0, output the whole string up to the terminating NUL. If *precision* is given, output up to (*precision*) characters
e	floating	convert to the format $<->$m.pppe$<\pm>$xx. The number of p's is determined by *precision* (default: 6)
f	floating	convert to the format $<->$mmmm.ppp. The number of ps is determined by *precision* (default: 6)
g	floating	convert to d, e or f format, whichever is shortest. Suppress insignificant zeros
%	—	output the character %

Δ Only lower-case *conversion-characters* are portable.

The scan control string contains ordinary non-whitespace characters, which must match the corresponding characters in the input stream, and optional scan specifications which correspond to the list of optional input targets in Slst; see Table 7 on p. 61. There must be exactly one target for each scan specification, except if the assignment suppressor * is used in a specification. Whitespace characters in the scan control string match optional whitespace characters in the input, so

scanf("let x =%d",&d);

matches

let x = 12 or **letx=12**

but not

le tx=12

Line boundaries are normally ignored, since the newline character is whitespace. Leading whitespace is normally skipped.

Strings are terminated by whitespace, Δ but this may be changed with the **[**scanset**]** conversion code. The scanset is a sequence of characters. If the first character is the circumflex ^ , the scanset is the set of all characters which are not in the subsequent sequence of characters. A character range may be specified with the construct first-last, e.g. **[0-9]**.

Table 7 *Scan specification*

A scan specification has the form:

% <*><*width*> scan-character

*   causes the field to be interpreted, but no assignment
     is made. No corresponding argument appears in the
     argument list
width indicates the maximum field width

The possible *scan-characters* are given below.

Argument:

Char	Pointer To	Action
d	int	expects a decimal integer in the input
o	int	expects an octal integer (with optional leading 0) in the input
x	int	expects a hexadecimal integer (with optional leading 0x) in the input
c	char	expects a single character without skipping whitespace. To obtain the first non-whitespace character, use %1s
s	char[]	expects a character string. The argument should be a pointer to an array of characters large enough to hold the string and a terminating NUL, which is added
e or f	float	a floating point number is expected. The format expected for floating point numbers is that given on p. 9, except that a unary plus is also allowed

Table 7 *Scan specification (continued)*

Char Pointer To Action

ld	long
lo	long
1x	long
le or double	
lf	double

the letter 'l' may be used to indicate that the corresponding argument is pointer to an object of type **long** instead of type **int**, or that it is a pointer to a **double** instead of a pointer to a **float**

hd	short
ho	short
hx	short

Δ some implementations use the letter 'h' to indicate that the corresponding argument points to an object of type **short** instead of **int**

[*scanset*]
  char[] Δ is the same as s (string), but skipping over leading spaces is suppressed and the string may contain only characters in *scanset*

Δ Only lower-case *scan characters* are portable.

Identifiers to avoid

The identifiers shown in Table 8 should be avoided because they are keywords or macros on some compilers. Keywords are marked with (k).

Table 8 *Identifiers to avoid*

abs	getchar	max
asm (k)	globaldef (k)	min
assert	globalref (k)	near (k)
auto (k)	globalvalue (k)	putc
break (k)	goto (k)	putchar
calloc	huge	readonly (k)
case (k)	if (k)	realloc
char (k)	int (k)	register (k)
clearerr	isalnum	return (k)
continue (k)	isalpha	short (k)
default (k)	isascii	sizeof (k)
do (k)	iscntrl	static (k)
double (k)	iscsym	stderr
else (k)	iscsymf	stdin
entry (k)	isdigit	stdout
enum (k)	isgraph	struct (k)
extern (k)	islower	switch (k)
far (k)	isprint	tm
feof	ispunct	toascii
ferror	isspace	tolower
fileno	isupper	toupper
float (k)	isxdigit	typedef (k)
for (k)	long (k)	union (k)
fortran (k)	mallinfo	unsigned (k)
free	malloc	void (k)
getc	mallopt	while (k)

Table 9 *Library functions by group*

General	*Conversion*	*Named files*	*Stream files*
abort	**atof**	**access**	**clearerr**
execl	**atoi**	**chdir**	**fclose**
exit	**atol**	**chmod**	**fdopen**
longjmp	**sprintf**	**mktemp**	**feof**
perror	**sscanf**	**unlink**	**ferror**
qsort	**swab**		**fflush**
setjmp		*System files*	**fgetc**
system	*Maths*	**close**	**fgets**
	abs	**creat**	**fileno**
Memory	**acos**	**fdopen**	**fopen**
calloc	**asin**	**fileno**	**fprintf**
free	**atan**	**lseek**	**fputc**
malloc	**atan2**	**open**	**fputs**
realloc	**ceil**	**read**	**fread**
	cos	**write**	**freopen**
Character	**exp**		**fscanf**
isathing	**fabs**		**fseek**
toascii	**floor**		**ftell**
tolower	**frexp**		**fwrite**
toupper	**hypot**		**getc**
	ldexp		**getw**
String	**log**		**putc**
index	**log10**		**putw**
rindex	**modf**		**rewind**
sprintf	**pow**		**setbuf**
sscanf	**rand**		**ungetc**
strcat	**sin**		
strchr	**sqrt**		*Standard*
strcmp	**srand**		*output*
strcpy	**tan**		*stream*
strlen	**tanh**		**getchar**
strncat			**gets**
strncmp			**printf**
strncpy			**putchar**
strrchr			**puts**
			scanf

Alphabetic list of library functions

void **abort**()

library   function   —
△ KR CR DR LAT DES

ABORT terminates a process forcibly, usually for debugging purposes. If possible, all open files are closed and a core dump is generated. The **abort** function does not normally return.

int **abs**(x)
int x=−123;

library   macro   stdio.h
△ KR CR CI

ABS returns the absolute value of its integer argument. It is sometimes implemented as the macro

#define abs(x) ((x)<0 ? (−(x)) : (x))

in stdio.h. Use **fabs** for floating variables. Your library may have an equivalent function **labs** for long integers.

The return value may not be correct for the largest negative **int**; for instance, if the size of an integer were 8 bits, **abs(−128)** might return −128. Some implementations trap this error.

int **access**(Fpath,amode)
system   function   —
Δ KR CR CI CC LAT DES

int amode=2;

ACCESS checks the accessibility of the named file. If **amode** is 0, Δ the existence of the file is checked, otherwise **amode** is a bit map as follows:

1 Δ   execute (search, if path is a directory)
2   write
4   read

The function returns 0 if the requested access is permitted; otherwise it returns −1 and sets **errno** to the appropriate error.

double **acos**(r)
math   function   math.h
Δ KR CR DR LAT

double r;

ACOS returns the arc cosine of r, which is measured in radians. If r is not in the range [−1 . . . 1], **acos** returns zero and sets **errno** to EDOM. The return value is in the range 0 to π.

66

double **asin**(r)

double r;

                math   function   math.h

                                            △ KR CR DR LAT

ASIN returns the arc sine of r, which is measured in radians. If r is not in the range $[-1 \ldots 1]$, **asin** returns zero and sets **errno** to EDOM. The return value is in the range $-\pi/2$ to $\pi/2$.

double **atan**(r)

double r;

                math   function   math.h

                                            △ KR CR DR LAT

ATAN returns the arc tangent of r, which is measured in radians. The return value is in the range $-\pi/2$ to $\pi/2$.

double **atan2**(x,y)

double x,y;

                math   function   math.h

                                      △ KR CR DR LAT DES

ATAN2 returns the arctangent of y/x. The return value is in the range $-\pi$ to π; the sign of both arguments is used to determine the quadrant. If x is zero, zero is returned and △ **errno** is set to EDOM.

double **atof**(s)

char *s;

ATOF converts the string of characters s into a **double**. Conversion ends with the first unrecognized character. Whitespace may precede the character representation of the **float**. The format of floats is as given on p. 9, but a unary plus sign is allowed. There is no error or overflow indication.

library   function   —

△ CR LAT

int **atoi**(s)

char *s;

ATOI converts the string of characters s into an **int**. Conversion ends with the first unrecognized character. Whitespace may precede the character representation of the **int**. There is no error or overflow indication.

library   function   —

△ CR LAT

long **atol**(s)

char *s;

ATOL is identical to **atoi**, but converts the string into a **long**.

library   function   —

△ KR CR CI LAT

```
char *calloc(number,size)                          system    macro    malloc.h
int number, size;                                                        Δ CR
```

CALLOC allocates an area of memory, sufficient to hold **number** items of **size** bytes, and initializes it to 0. The returned pointer is guaranteed to be sufficiently aligned to hold an object of any type. If not enough memory is available, the NULL pointer is returned. The **calloc** function is typically used with the **sizeof** operator, as in

p=calloc(20, sizeof(int));

A faster (macro) version of **calloc** may exist in malloc.h.

```
double ceil(x)                                       math     function   math.h
double x;                                                          Δ KR CR DR LAT DES
```

CEIL returns (as a **double**) the smallest integer that is not less than its argument. (Compare **floor**.)

int **chdir**(Dpath)

CHDIR changes the current working directory. It returns zero if the directory has been changed successfully, otherwise −1.

The working directory is the directory used for files whose name does not begin with the root indicator /. This function makes sense only on systems with a tree directory structure.

int **chmod**(Fpath,pmode)
int pmode=0600;

CHMOD changes the file protection of a file. It returns zero if successful, otherwise −1. The user must have write permission for the file. On UNIX, **pmode** is a bit map of privileges which includes the following:

0400 owner, read	0040 group, read	0004 world, read
0200 owner, write	0020 group, write	0002 world, write
0100 owner, execute	0010 group, execute	0001 world, execute

A write privilege implies a delete privilege.

70

void **clearerr**(StreamP)

library   macro   stdio.h
△ KR CR LAT DES

CLEARERR resets the error indication for StreamP, so that **ferror** ceases to indicate an error. Error indications persist until **clearerr** is called or the stream is closed.

int **close**(Handle)

system   function   —
△ CC

CLOSE closes the file associated with the Handle. If the file was open for writing, any buffered characters are written out first. The function returns zero if it has closed the file successfully, otherwise − 1. △ The cause of the error may be in **errno**.

double **cos**(r)
double r;

math   function   math.h
△ KR CR LAT

COS returns the cosine of its argument, which is measured in radians. The return value is in the range [−1 . . . 1].

int **creat**(Fpath,pmode)   system   function   –
int pmode=0400;   Δ CC

CREAT creates a new file. If a file of the same name exists already, it may be truncated. The **creat** function returns a small positive **int** (the file Handle) if it can create the file, otherwise −1. If the file is created, **pmode** determines its access privileges (see **chmod**).

Be prepared for aggravation on systems which require a distinction between translated and untranslated files. You may have to supply a third argument, a **pmode** translation indicator bit, a different function name, a separate **extern** variable, or a different linking procedure to **creat** or **open** a binary file. Or it may be altogether impossible to **creat** a file with the desired mode. Chaos rules O.K.

72

int **execl**(Fpath,*arglist*,(char*)0)

system   function   —
Δ KR CR CI CC LAT DES

EXECL executes (chains to) the program specified by Fpath. If successful, the function does not return and control is passed to the specified program. If unsuccessful, the function returns −1 and **errno** indicates the reason. Where applicable, the chained process inherits the parent's environment. *Arglist* consists of zero or more pointers to string arguments which are passed to the **main** function of the chained process, as in

execl("cat", "file.1", "file.2", (char*)0);

void **exit**(status)
int status = 0;

standard   function   —

EXIT terminates the process from which it is called. The specified status (which may be omitted altogether) is passed to the calling process (for instance, the shell or command interpreter). By convention, a return status of zero signifies successful completion; any other return status signifies an error. Any open files are flushed and closed first; **_exit** circumvents these cleanup actions. Falling off the edge of the **main** function is equivalent to calling **exit(0)**.

double **exp**(p)
double p;

math   function   math.h
△ KR CR LAT

EXP returns the constant e raised to the power of the argument p. If overflow occurs, **exp** may return a huge value and △ sets **errno** to ERANGE. This function may be written as

pow(2.718281828459045,p)

double **fabs**(x)
double x;

math   function   math.h
△ KR CR LAT

FABS returns the absolute value of x. Some implementations allow the **abs** macro to be used for this purpose (not recommended, unless you define it yourself).

int **fclose**(StreamP)

standard   function   stdio.h

FCLOSE closes the file StreamP. Any associated buffers are flushed first, and buffers allocated by the I/O system are deallocated. The return value is zero if the file has been closed successfully, otherwise EOF. Files should be closed even if they were only open for reading. All open files are automatically closed when **exit** is called.

FILE *fdopen(Handle,rwa)   library   function   stdio.h
char *rwa;   △ KR CR CI CC LAT DES
FDOPEN associates a stream pointer with a file Handle. This allows functions such as **putc**
access to a file previously opened with calls such as **open**. The first argument is the file handle
obtained by **open** or **creat**; the second is a pointer to a string analogous to the **rwa** argument
of **fopen**; it must agree with the **mode** with which the file has been **opened**. Use of this function
should be avoided. (Compare **fileno**.)

int **feof**(StreamP)   standard   macro   stdio.h
                                                                    △ CR CI DES
FEOF returns non-zero if the end-of-file has been read on StreamP. It returns 0 if end-of-file has
not been reached.

int **ferror**(StreamP)

standard   macro   stdio.h
Δ CR DES

FERROR tests whether an error has occurred while reading or writing to a stream. It returns 0 if no error has occurred, otherwise non-zero. The error indication persists until it is cleared with **clearerr** or the stream is closed. This macro is most useful to test successful completion of functions such as **getw** which cannot reliably indicate errors.

int **fflush**(StreamP)

standard   function   stdio.h
Δ CR DES

FFLUSH flushes any information buffered for StreamP. Output files are normally buffered, unless they are connected to a terminal. If an error occurs, the function returns EOF.

int **fgetc**(StreamP)

standard   function   stdio.h
Δ CR

FGETC returns the next character from StreamP; it may use **malloc** to allocate a buffer if this is the first I/O request to StreamP. It returns EOF on end-of-file or error. Characters from a terminal device are not normally available until the end-of-line is reached. Use **fgetc** in preference to **getc** if program size is important.

```
char *fgets(b,maxb,StreamP)                          standard   function   stdio.h
char b[100];
int maxb=100;
```
FGETS reads a line from the stream StreamP. It reads maxb−1 characters, or up to the newline character, whichever comes first. In the latter case, b will include the terminating newline (\n). A NUL is appended to the characters read. If you attempt to read past the end-of-file, or if an error occurs, **fgets** may return the NULL pointer; otherwise it returns its first argument.

int **fileno**(StreamP)   standard   macro   stdio.h
                                                                 Δ CR CI CC DES

FILENO returns the integer file Handle associated with the specified stream pointer. Be warned that many systems do not allow access to the same file by StreamP and Handle.

double **floor**(x)   math   function   math.h
                                                                 Δ KR CR DR LAT DES

FLOOR returns, as a **double**, the largest integer that is not greater than its argument. (Compare **ceil**.)

77

FILE *fopen(Fpath,rwa)   standard function stdio.h
char *rwa;

FOPEN opens a file and returns a file pointer to the stream associated with it. If **fopen** cannot open the file, it returns the NULL pointer. Typically, no buffer is allocated at this stage; buffers are allocated by the first **getc** or **putc** calls.

The access mode is specified by **rwa** and is officially one of the following:

"r" opens a file for reading. The file is positioned at the beginning-of-file

"w" opens a file for writing only. The file is created if it does not exist. If a file of the same name exists, it may be truncated

"a" opens a file for appending. This is identical to "w", but data is appended at the end-of-file.

It is illegal to read from files which are open in modes "w" or "a", or to write to files open in mode "r". Some systems therefore have additional modes:

Δ "r+" opens a file for reading and positions it at the beginning-of-file, but writing is also allowed

Δ "w+" opens a file for writing, but reading is also allowed

Δ "a+" opens a file for appending, but reading is also allowed

78

Where reading and writing is allowed, an intervening **fseek** or **rewind** is required between different operations.

To make matters worse, systems which require file translation may have yet more modes which may be combined with the above:

Δ "rb" or "r+b" opens a file for untranslated reading
Δ "wb" or "w+b" opens a file for untranslated writing

Sadly, other methods to indicate the type of access are also used.

int **fprintf**(StreamP,Pfmt,Plst)   standard   function   stdio.h

FPRINTF performs formatted output to StreamP. It returns the number of characters actually printed; an error has occurred if the return value is −1. *See p. 57* for details of its arguments.

int **fputc**(c,StreamP)   standard   function   stdio.h

char c;   Δ CR

FPUTC writes a single character to StreamP; it may use **malloc** to allocate a buffer if this is the first I/O request to StreamP. It returns the character, or EOF on error. Use **fputc** in preference to **putc** if program size is important.

void **fputs**(s,StreamP)   standard   function   stdio.h
char *s;

FPUTS writes the string s to the specified stream. It does not append a newline (\n) to the string.

There is no return value. This function is equivalent to **fprintf(StreamP, "%s",s)**

int **fread**(p,bytes,number,StreamP)   standard   function   stdio.h
                                                                  Δ CR
char *p;
int bytes, number;

FREAD reads the specified **number** of items of a given size (**bytes**) into storage beginning at p. The items are read from the stream StreamP, and the number of items actually read is returned. EOF or zero are returned for errors; in this case, the last item may be incomplete. The stream must normally have been opened in binary mode. This function is used to read items written with **fwrite**.

void **free**(m)   library   macro   malloc.h
char *m;

FREE frees an area of memory previously allocated with **malloc**, **calloc** or **realloc**. A faster (macro) version of **free** may exist in malloc.h.

```c
FILE *freopen(Fpath,rwa,StreamP)
char *rwa;
```

standard function stdio.h

△ CR CI DES

FREOPEN closes the stream associated with StreamP and then substitutes the file specified by Fpath, i.e. it executes **fopen(Fpath,rwa)**. The function returns its third argument (the stream pointer) if successful, otherwise it returns a NULL pointer. A typical use is to associate one of the predefined names **stdin**, **stdout** and **stderr** with a file, as in

if (freopen("out.log","a",stdout)) . . .

Since **stdout** is a constant, a combination of **fclose** and **fopen** could not have been used, unless it were assumed that an **fopen** automatically returns the stream pointer released by the last **fclose**.

```c
double frexp(x,pi)
double x;
int *pi;
```

library function —

△ KR CR DR LAT DES

FREXP separates a floating point value into mantissa and exponent. It returns the mantissa with magnitude [0.5 . . . [1.0. The exponent is stored in the int pointed to by **pi**. Therefore, if

81

mant=frexp(x,pi);

then

mant*2.0 (*pi)

is the original value.

int **fscanf**(StreamP,Sfmt,Slst)   standard   function   stdio.h

FSCANF performs formatted input from StreamP. It returns EOF if the end-of-file has been read; otherwise it returns the number of successfully matched and converted input items. See p. 57 for details of its arguments.

int **fseek**(StreamP,off,whence)   standard   function   stdio.h

long off;

int whence;

FSEEK positions the stream StreamP to a specified byte offset in the file. It returns 0 if successful, EOF for improper seeks. The offset **off** is measured from a location named by **whence,** which may be

82

0   from the beginning of the file

Δ 1   from the current read/write position

Δ 2   from the end of the file

Seeking may not work as expected on non-UNIX file systems; on such systems, **fseek** should be used only to seek to absolute locations (**whence=0**) previously returned by **ftell**. The fseek function destroys any character pushed back with **ungetc**. The result is undefined on devices (terminals, printers) not capable of seeking.

long **ftell**(StreamP)   standard   function   stdio.h

Δ CR DES

FTELL returns the current byte offset of the specified stream file, measured from the beginning of the file. It returns −1L on error. On systems with file translation, the return value is only useful for **fseek**.

int **fwrite**(p,bytes,number,StreamP)   standard   function   stdio.h
char *p;   △ CR
int bytes, number;
FWRITE writes the specified **number** of items of size **bytes** to the (untranslated) stream
StreamP, starting in storage at location **p**. It returns the number of bytes actually written, 0 if there
is an error. The **fread** function is normally used to read items written by **fwrite**.

int **getc**(StreamP)   standard   macro   stdio.h
GETC returns the next character from StreamP; it may use **malloc** to allocate a buffer if this is the
first I/O request to StreamP. It returns EOF on end-of-file or error. Use **getc** in preference to
fgetc if speed is important.

int **getchar**()   standard   macro   stdio.h
GETCHAR is equivalent to **getc**(**stdin**). Characters from a terminal device are not normally
available until the end-of-line.

char *gets(b)
char b[1000];

library   function   stdio.h
Δ KR CR CI

GETS reads a line from the standard input stream and places it in b. A NUL is appended to the line; the terminating newline is not included. The buffer b must be large enough to hold the string. A NULL pointer is returned on end-of-file or error, otherwise **gets** returns its argument.

int **getw**(StreamP)

standard   function   stdio.h
Δ CR LAT

GETW reads a binary **int** from StreamP and returns that **int**. The exact number of bytes read depends on the size of an **int** in the implementation. EOF is returned on error, but as this is a perfectly good **int**, **ferror** and **feof** should be used to detect errors. Where applicable, StreamP must have been opened in binary mode. Use the function **getw** to read back a value written by **putw**. Equivalent functions **getl** and **putl** may exist for **long** integers.

double **hypot**(x,y)
double x,y;

math   function   math.h
Δ KR CR CI DR LAT DES

HYPOT returns the value of **sqrt(x*x+y*y)**.

char * **index**(s,c)
INDEX is identical to **strchr**, which is preferred.

	library	function	—
	standard	macro	ctype.h
int **isathing**(char)			Δ CR
int **isalnum**(c)		٢	
int **isalpha**(c)			
int **isascii**(c)			Δ CR
int **iscntrl**(c)			Δ CR
int **isdigit**(c)			
int **islower**(c)			
int **isprint**(c)			Δ CR
int **ispunct**(c)			Δ CR
int **isspace**(c)			
int **isupper**(c)			

IS*ATHING* are macros which return non-zero integers if the character argument is in a certain class of characters. The return value of **isascii** is defined for any **int**. All other macros are only defined if **isascii(c)** is true, unless **c** is EOF. Table 10 illustrates treatment of these macros; be warned that minor disagreements do exist.

Table 10 *The isathing macros*

Range	alnum	alpha	ascii	cntrl	lower	print	punct	space	upper
0 … 8	○	○	●	●	○	○	○	○	○
0x9 (\t)	○	○	●	●	○	○	○	●	○
0xa (\n)	○	○	●	●	○	○	○	●	○
0xb (\v)	○	○	●	●	○	○	○	●	○
0xc (\f)	○	○	●	●	○	○	○	●	○
0xd (\r)	○	○	●	●	○	○	○	●	○
0xe–0x1f	○	○	●	●	○	○	○	○	○
Space	○	○	●	○	○	●	○	●	○
!"#$%&()*+,−./	○	○	●	○	○	●	●	○	○
'0'…'9'	●	○	●	○	○	●	○	○	○
:;<=>?@	○	○	●	○	○	●	●	○	○
'A'…'Z'	●	●	●	○	○	●	○	○	●
[\]^_`	○	○	●	○	○	●	●	○	○
'a'…'z'	●	●	●	○	●	●	○	○	○

Table 10 *The isathing macros (continued)*

Range	alnum	alpha	ascii	cntrl	lower	print	punct	space	upper
~{|}	○	○	●	○	○	●	●	○	○
0x7f (DEL)	○	○	●	●	○	○	○	○	○
0x80...	?	?	○	?	?	?	?	?	?
EOF	○	○	○	○	○	○	○	○	○

library	function	math.h
	△ KR CR DR LAT DES	

double **ldexp**(x,y)
double x;
int y;

LDEXP returns x multiplied by two to the power of y. It may be written as **x * pow (2.0, (double) y)**. Errors may occur on underflow or overflow and △ set **errno** to ERANGE. (Compare **frexp**.)

double **log**(x)
double x;

math   function   math.h
                            Δ KR CR LAT

LOG returns the natural (base e) logarithm of the argument. If x is zero or negative, the return value is undefined and Δ **errno** is set to EDOM.

double **log10**(x)
double x;

math   function   math.h
                            Δ KR CR LAT

LOG10 returns the base 10 logarithm of the argument. If x is zero or negative, its value is undefined and Δ **errno** is set to EDOM.

int **longjmp**(env,retv)
jmp_buf env;
int retv;

library   function   setjmp.h

LONGJMP restores the environment set up by the last call to **setjmp**. It returns to **setjmp** as if that function had just returned with the value **retv**. *See* **setjmp** (p. 98) for a sample program.

89

long **lseek** (Handle,off,whence) system   function   –
long off;   Δ CC
int whence;
LSEEK positions a file to an arbitrary position, measured in bytes (**off**) from

   the beginning of the file,   if **whence** is 0
   Δ the current position,   if **whence** is 1
   Δ the end-of-file,   if **whence** is 2

The function returns the new pointer location (measured from the beginning of the file), or –1L if an illegal seek is attempted. Treatment of seeks beyond the end-of-file is not reliable. Seeking to positions other than those previously obtained with **lseek** is unreliable in the case of translated files.

char ***malloc**(bytes)   standard   macro   malloc.h
unsigned bytes;   Δ CR
MALLOC allocates an area of memory of size **bytes**. It returns a pointer to the first byte, which is aligned sufficiently to hold any object. The area is not initialized. A NULL pointer is returned if there is no space available.

char *__mktemp__(template)
char template[] = "krXXXXXX";

MKTEMP generates a unique filename from a template. The six trailing X's are replaced by a unique series of characters. The function replaces the template and returns the pointer to it; the pointer will point to an empty string if a unique filename could not be created.

library   function   —
Δ KR CR CI CC LAT DES

double __modf__(x,intptr)
double x;
double *intptr;

MODF returns the positive fractional part of x and stores the integral part through __intptr__.

library   function   —
Δ KR CR DR LAT DES

int __open__(Fpath,mode)
int mode;

OPEN opens a file and returns a file Handle. The __mode__ is one of the following:

system   function   —
Δ CC

0 open file for reading
1 open file for writing
2 open file for updating (reading and writing)

91

If the file cannot be opened, **open** returns −1, otherwise the return value is a small positive integer which is the file descriptor. The file is positioned at the beginning-of-file. This function suffers from defects similar to **creat** (see p. 72).

library function —
△ KR CR CI CC LAT DES

void **perror**(s)

char ∗s=''oops'';

PERROR prints a short error message to **stderr** describing the last error encountered during a call to the library. The last error is obtained from **errno**. The **perror** function is equivalent to

fprintf(stderr, ''%s: %s\n'' ,s,sys_errlist[errno])

double **pow**(x,y)

math function math.h
△ KR CR DR LAT

double x,y;

POW returns x raised to the power of y. A huge number is returned on overflow, and △ **errno** is set to ERANGE. If both x and y are zero, **pow** returns 0. If y is negative and non-integral, the result is undefined and △ **errno** is set to EDOM.

92

int **printf**(Pfmt,Plst)   standard   function   stdio.h

PRINTF performs formatted output to the standard output stream. It returns the number of characters actually printed; an error has occurred if the return value is − 1. *See* p. 57 for details of its arguments.

int **putc**(c,StreamP)   standard   macro   stdio.h

char c;

PUTC writes a single character to StreamP; it may use **malloc** to allocate a buffer if this is the first I/O request to StreamP. It returns the character, or EOF on error. Use **putc** in preference to **fputc** if speed is important.

int **putchar**(c)   standard   macro   stdio.h

char c;

PUTCHAR is equivalent to **putc(c,stdout)**.

int **puts**(s)   library   function   stdio.h
                                                                                     △ KR CR
char *s;

PUTS writes a character string (excluding the terminating NUL) to **stdout**, followed by a newline. The function is equivalent to **printf("%s\n",s)**.

int **putw**(x,StreamP)   standard   function   stdio.h
int x;   Δ CR LAT

PUTW writes a number of characters which are the binary representation of x to the stream
StreamP. It returns EOF on error but, as this is a perfectly good integer, errors should be checked
with **ferror**. The stream must be binary. The function **getw** should be used to read the **int** from
the stream. Files created with **putw** are not portable across systems.

void **qsort**(base,nel,bytes,compar)   library   function   —
unsigned nel; char *base;   Δ KR CR VAX MC LAT
int bytes;
int (* compar) ();

QSORT implements a quick-sort algorithm to sort an array of **nel** elements beginning at **base**.
The size of each element is **bytes**. The comparison is carried out by the function pointed to by
compar; the comparison function is passed pointers to the two elements to compare, and must
return

  0   if first==second
 −1   if first<second
  1   if first>second

94

For instance, the following sorts an array of pointers:

```
char *aps[] = {"hello","world","goodbye","world" };
int i;
compar (a,b)
char **a, **b;
{
    return (strcmp(*a,*b));
}
main()
{
    qsort(aps,4,sizeof(char *),compar);
    for (i=0;i<4;i++)
        printf("%s ",aps[i]);
}
```

and results in **goodbye hello world world** on the output stream.

int **rand**()

RAND returns a positive pseudorandom **int**. It is unwise to rely on the distribution or period of the generated numbers. (*See also* **srand**.)

```
int read(Handle,b,bytes)
char b[100];
int bytes=100;
```

READ attempts to read the specified number of bytes from the file. It returns the number of bytes actually read. This may be less than **bytes** if input is from a terminal (only one line may be read) or if the file is translated. A return value of 0 means end-of-file, EOF that an error has occurred.

```
char *realloc(p,bytes)
char *p;
int bytes;
```

REALLOC changes the size of the area pointed to by p to the number of **bytes** specified. It returns a pointer to the new area. It is free to move the original area, so pointers to objects within it will be invalid.

int **rewind**(StreamP)   standard   function   stdio.h
△ CR CI

REWIND resets the read/write position for the stream StreamP to the beginning-of-file. It returns EOF if an error has occurred. This is the same as **fseek(StreamP,0L,0)**. It destroys any character pushed back by **ungetc.**

rindex(s,c)   library   function   —
RINDEX is identical to **strrchr**, which is preferred.

int **scanf**(Sfmt,Slst)   standard   function   stdio.h

SCANF performs formatted input from the standard input stream **stdin**. It returns EOF if the end-of-file has been read; otherwise it returns the number of successfully matched and converted input items. *See p. 57 for details of its arguments.*

setbuf(StreamP,buf)
  standard   function   stdio.h
                                      △ CR CI DES
char *buf=NULL;

SETBUF associates the buffer pointed to by **buf** with the stream StreamP. If StreamP is NULL, the file will be unbuffered. Otherwise the size of the buffer must be of size BUFSIZ (a constant defined in stdio.h) or bigger. This function should be used after a file has been opened, but before any I/O has been performed on it.

int **setjmp**(env)
  library   function   setjmp.h
                                  △ KR CR CI LAT
jmp_buf env;

SETJMP sets up a non-local goto by saving the calling function's environment in an aggregate whose type (**jmp_buf**) is defined in <setjmp.h>. It returns 0 when first called. It will appear to return again if **longjmp** is called. The following example illustrates its use:

```
#include <setjmp.h>
#include <stdio.h>
jmp_buf savenv;
main()
{

    switch(setjmp(savenv))
    {

        case 0:submarin();
               break;
        case 1:printf("Can't find water\n");
               break;
    }
}

submarin()
{

    FILE * fp;
    if (fp=fopen("water.fil","r"))
    {
```

```
        /* read water.fil, then */
        fclose(fp);
    }
    else
    {
        /* could not open water.fil */
        longjmp(savenv,1);
    }
}
```

```
double sin(r)
double r;
```

math   function   math.h
                    △ KR CR LAT

SIN returns the sine of r, which is given in radians. The return value is in the range $[-1 \ldots 1]$.

int **sprintf**(s,Pfmt,Plst)
char s[100];
SPRINTF performs formatted output to the character array s. It returns the number of characters actually printed (excluding the terminating NUL); an error has occurred if the return value is −1. See p. 57 for details of its arguments.

standard   function   —

double **sqrt**(x)
double x;
SQRT returns the square root of its argument. If x is negative, it returns zero and Δ sets **errno** to EDOM.

math   function   math.h
Δ KR CR LAT

void **srand**(seed)
int seed;
SRAND seeds the random number generator **rand** with the starting point **seed**. If **seed** is an implementation-dependent number (like 1 or 5), **srand** reinitializes the random number generator.

library   function   —
Δ KR CR CI CC LAT

101

int **sscanf**(s,Sfmt,Slst)   standard   function   stdio.h

char *s;

SSCANF performs formatted input from the string s. It returns EOF if the terminating NUL has
been read; otherwise it returns the number of successfully matched and converted input items.
See p. 57 for details of its arguments.

char ***strcat**(d,s)   library   function   string.h
                                                                                       △ CR
char *d, *s;

STRCAT appends the string s to the string d. Both strings must be NUL terminated. It returns its first
argument. String d must be big enough to accommodate the result. The call **strcat(d,d)** may
cause havoc.

char ***strchr**(s,c)   library   function   string.h
                                                                                       △ KR CR LAT
char *s="find Me";

char c='M';

STRCHR finds the first occurrence of character c in string s. It returns the NULL pointer if the
character was not found; otherwise a pointer to the position of the first occurrence of the
character. (The function **index** does the same.)

int **strcmp**(s1,s2)   library   function   string.h
char ∗s1, ∗s2;
STRCMP compares two strings. It returns an integer which represents the lexicographical
comparison of the two strings, and is

negative   if s1 is less than or shorter than s2
0   if s1 is equal to s2
positive   if s1 is greater than or longer than s2

This function may use signed comparison of characters.

char ∗**strcpy**(db,s)   library   function   string.h
char db[100];
char ∗s=''to be copied'';
STRCPY copies the string s to **db**. It stops after it has copied the terminating NUL of s. The buffer
db must be big enough to accommodate the result. It returns its first argument.

int **strlen**(s)

char *s;

STRLEN returns the length of string s, excluding the terminating NUL character.

char ***strncat**(d,s,mx)

char *d, *s;

int mx;

STRNCAT appends the string s to the string d, using up to **mx** characters from the source string s. String d must be and string s probably should be NUL terminated. String d must be big enough to contain d and s. It returns its first argument.

int **strncmp**(s1,s2,mx)

char *s1, *s2;

int mx;

STRNCMP compares two strings. It returns an integer which represents the lexicographical comparison (see **strcmp**). The argument **mx** gives the maximum number of characters to be compared. This function may use signed comparison of characters.

```
char *strncpy(db,s,mx)                                              library    function    string.h
char db[100];                                                                          Δ KR CR LAT
char *s="Hello, World";
int mx=100;
STRNCPY copies the string s to d, up to the number of characters specified in mx. It returns its first
argument. If mx characters are copied, the result will not be NUL-terminated.


strrchr(s,c)                                                        library    function    string.h
char *s;                                                                               Δ KR CR LAT
char c;
STRRCHR returns a pointer to the last occurrence of the character c in the null-terminated string s.
If the character is not found, it returns the NULL pointer. (Same as rindex.)


void swab(s,d,bytes)                                                        library    function    —
char *s, *d;                                                                        Δ KR CR VAX CI LAT DES
int bytes;
SWAB copies the number of bytes indicated (which must be even) from the source s to the
destination d, exchanging adjacent even and odd bytes.
```

int **system**(s)

char *s="ps − 1";

standard function —
△ VAX CI DR LAT DES

SYSTEM causes a copy of the shell to be executed as if the string s had been typed at the terminal. The return value is the value returned by the shell; it is non-zero if an error occurred.

Although part of the standard I/O library, this function is not easily implemented on systems other than UNIX and is often omitted.

double **tan**(r)

double r;

math function math.h
△ KR CR LAT U7

TAN returns the tangent of its argument, which is measured in radians. A huge number is returned if r is at a singular point (. . . −3π/2, −π/2, π/2, 3π/2 . . .) and △ **errno** is set to ERANGE.

double **tanh**(r)

double r;

math function math.h
△ KR CR CI DR LAT DES

TANH returns the hyperbolic tangent of its argument, which is measured in radians.

106

int **toascii**(c)

                                        standard   macro   ctype.h

                                                △ KR CR CI CC LAT DES U7

    int c;

TOASCII turns the character or integer c into an ASCII character in the range 0 . . . 0x7f. It is not portable to machines which do not use the ASCII character set. It clobbers the value EOF, which should be tested before using **toascii**.

int **tolower**(c)

                                          standard   macro   ctype.h

    char c;

TOLOWER returns the lower-case equivalent of the upper-case character c. The result is undefined if c is not an upper-case character; you must write

if (isupper(c)) c=tolower(c);

unless you know for sure that c is upper case. Only

if (isascii(c)) if (isupper(c)) c=tolower(c);

is totally safe.

int **toupper**(c)

standard   macro   ctype.h

TOUPPER returns the upper-case equivalent of the lower-case character c. (The comments on **tolower** apply.)

int **ungetc**(c,StreamP)

standard   function   stdio.h

char c;

UNGETC writes ('pushes back') a character to the buffer of the input StreamP so that the character will be the next to be returned by the **getc** family of calls. EOF should never be pushed back. You must previously have read something from the stream. A single level of push-back is guaranteed, but only if a character has previously been read from StreamP. The function returns the character, or EOF if the push-back has failed.

int **unlink**(Fpath)

system   function   –
△ VAX

UNLINK removes a link from the file specified. On non-UNIX systems, this is equivalent to deleting the file; VAX commendably uses a **delete** function instead. Zero is returned if successful, otherwise −1. The file is destroyed only when the last link to it is broken. It may be advisable to construct your own **delete** and **rename** functions.

```
int write(Handle,b,bytes)
char b[100];
int bytes = 100;
```

WRITE writes the specified number of bytes from the buffer b to the file specified. If successful, it returns the number of bytes actually written. It is an error if less bytes were written than requested. On error, it returns −1.

Index

112

Computer Handbooks

Languages

Assembly Language for the 8086 and 8088
   Robert Erskine
C Language   Friedman Wagner-Dobler

Business Applications

VisiCalc   Peter Gosling

Microcomputers

The Apricot   Peter Gosling
The Sinclair QL   Guy Langdon and
   David Heckingbottom

Operating Systems

Introduction to Operating Systems
   Lawrence Blackburn and Marcus Taylor

Pocket Guides

Programming

Programming   John Shelley
BASIC   Roger Hunt
COBOL   Ray Welland
FORTH   Steven Vickers
FORTRAN   Philip Ridler
FORTRAN 77   Clive Page
LOGO   Boris Allan
Pascal   David Watt

Assembly Languages

Assembly Language for the 6502   Bob Bright
Assembly Language for the 8085   Noel Morris
Assembly Language for the MC 68000 Series
   Robert Erskine
Assembly Language for the Z80   Julian Ullmann

Microcomputers

Acorn Electron   Neil Cryer and Pat Cryer
Commodore 64   Boris Allan
Programming for the Apple   John Gray
Programming for the BBC Micro   Neil Cryer
   and Pat Cryer
Sinclair Spectrum   Steven Vickers
The IBM PC   Peter Gosling

Operating Systems

CP/M   Lawrence Blackburn and Marcus Taylor
MS-DOS   Val King and Dick Waller
PC-DOS   Val King and Dick Waller
UNIX   Lawrence Blackburn and Marcus Taylor

Word Processors

Introduction to Word Processing   Maddie Labinger
IBM Displaywriter   Jacquelyne A. Morison
Philips P5020   Peter Flewitt
Wang System 5   Maddie Labinger
WordStar   Maddie Labinger

Notes

Notes